HISTORY RELIVED

The Victorians

Alison Cooper

Photographs by Martyn F. Chillmaid

WAYLAND

HISTORY RELIVED

This book is a differentiated text version of *The Victorians* by Liz Gogerly.

Conceived and produced for Wayland by

Nutshell
MEDIA

www.nutshellmedialtd.co.uk

This edition first published in 2009 by Wayland.

© Copyright 2009 Nutshell Media Ltd

Editor: Polly Goodman
Original designer: Simon Borrough
Layout for this edition: Jane Hawkins
All reconstructions set up and photographed by: Martyn F. Chillmaid
Photograph page 27: Alvey & Towers

British Library Cataloguing in Publication Data
Cooper, Alison, 1967-
The Victorians. -- Differentiated ed. -- (History relived)
1. Great Britain--History--Victoria, 1837-1901--Juvenile literature. 2. Great Britain--Social life and customs--19th century--Juvenile literature.
I. Title II. Series III. Gogerly, Liz. Victorians reconstructed.
941'.081-dc22

ISBN: 978 0 7502 5866 1

Printed and bound in China

Wayland is a division of Hachette Children's Books,
A Hachette UK Company

www.hachette.co.uk

Cover photographs:
Top left: A Victorian family pose for a photograph dressed in their best clothes;
Top centre: A woman throws some waste into the street;
Right: A girl wearing clothes that were typical in Victorian times;
Bottom: A woman puts the kettle on the range.

Title page: Victorian streets were often dirty with slops and horse dung.

The photographer wishes to thank the following for their help and assistance:

Black Country Living Museum, Dudley; Blist Hill Victorian Town; The Ironbridge Gorge Museum.

Contents

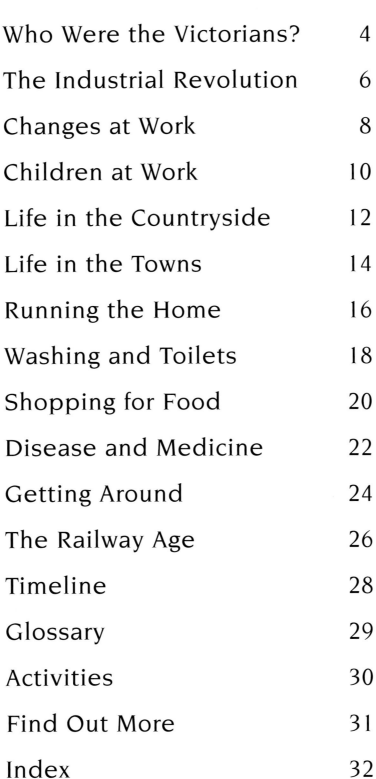

Who Were the Victorians?

▲ A Victorian family poses for a photograph.

sailor suit

lace gown

best hat

lace frills

cotton and lace shirt

waistcoat, jacket and tie

Victoria was just a teenager when she became queen in 1837. Her reign lasted for 64 years.

There are no photographs of Victoria as a girl because photography had not been invented at that time. There are photographs of her as a white-haired old lady, though. Photography was just one of many inventions during her long reign.

Queen Victoria married her cousin, Prince Albert, in 1840. They had nine children. Large families were very common in Victorian times.

There were great differences between rich and poor Victorian families. A few families were so rich that no one had to work.

In families that were not so rich, the father worked. He might have a job in an office. The mother ran the home and organized the servants. Children often spent most of their time with a nanny. They did not see much of their parents.

In poor families, the father and the older children went out to work. The mother might wash clothes for other families, as well as doing all the cooking, washing and cleaning for her own family. The younger children helped out.

▼ This girl has a *Girl's Own* annual. These were very popular in the late 1800s.

lace-up boots

frilled dress

Girl's Own annual

pinafore

high collar

ringlets

The Industrial Revolution

▲ A miner arrives for work at a coal mine.

Britain changed very quickly during the Industrial Revolution.

Steam engines that could be used to power machinery were invented. The steam engines needed coal to make them work. The coal was burned to heat water and turn it into steam.

miner

mine office

coal

winding gear

Coal came from mines. Miners dug deep tunnels to dig out the coal. It was hard, dangerous work.

Big factories had to be built for the new, steam-powered machines. People came to the factories to get jobs.

Steam was used to power ships, as well as factory machinery. But the first steam ships could not make very long journeys because they had to keep stopping to take on more coal. These ships were mainly used to carry loads around the coast. Wooden sailing ships carried British goods around the world for most of the nineteenth century.

In 1843, a great engineer called Isambard Kingdom Brunel built the first steamship made of iron. It was called *Great Britain*. This strong ship could make longer, faster voyages because it could carry more coal.

rope   rope fibre

barrel of tar   wooden boat

▼ These boatyard workers are rolling fibre into rope.

Changes at Work

When Victoria became queen, most people in Britain lived and worked in the countryside. During her reign, thousands of people moved to the towns to find work in the new factories.

In the busy towns, there was more work for craftsmen such as carpenters, tailors and shoemakers. New machinery was changing their jobs, as well. In the 1850s, a new type of sewing machine was invented. Shoemakers began to use these machines to make shoes more quickly.

▼ A shoemaker in his workshop.

lace-up boot

shoe last

sewing machine

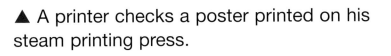
▲ A printer checks a poster printed on his steam printing press.

Printing was another industry that changed a lot in Victorian times. In the early 1800s, printers began to use printing presses that were powered by steam.

printer | poster

steam printing press | wooden letter blocks

Later, presses were invented that could print on both sides of the paper. They could use rolls of paper, too, instead of sheets. This meant that newspapers could be produced quickly and cheaply for the first time.

In 1851, the Victorians showed off their many new inventions at a show called the Great Exhibition. It was held in the Crystal Palace in London, an amazing glass and iron building like a giant greenhouse.

Children at Work

Children worked long hours and did some dangerous jobs in Victorian times.

In coal mines, small children worked in dark tunnels deep underground. Children worked in factories, too. Sometimes they had to crawl under moving machinery to clean it. Accidents were common.

▼ Two boys slowly push a wagon full of coal.

wagon

coal

iron tracks

entrance to mine

In Victorian times, there were many children without families to look after them. Some of these children went to work in the factories as apprentices. They lived in apprentice houses, which were set up by the factory owners for their apprentices.

Children worked as apprentices for seven years. Instead of being paid, they were given a place to live, food and clothes. They had some lessons, too, when they were not at work.

Many people were worried about the hard, dangerous work that children did. Laws were passed to protect child workers in the mines, mills and factories. The laws did not protect children working in small workshops, on farms and in other businesses, though. For these children, work was as hard as ever.

▲ Apprentices slept in dormitories like this one, in an apprentice house.

wooden bed   woollen blanket

chamber pot   candle lamp

broom   laundry basket

Life in the Countryside

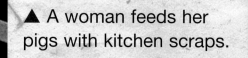
▲ A woman feeds her pigs with kitchen scraps.

pig sty

bucket of food

vegetable patch

cottage

Life in the countryside became harder for many people in Victorian times. New farm machinery meant that many workers lost their jobs. There were other big changes, too.

For hundreds of years people had farmed on common land. This was land they shared with their neighbours.

In the late 1700s and early 1800s, rich landowners took over the common land. People had to start paying rent to the landowners. Many people began working for the landowner instead, but they did not earn very much money.

Many poor families lived in small cottages. Seven or eight people might be crowded into just two rooms. They kept a few animals and grew vegetables for food.

Pigs were very useful because every part of the pig could be eaten. Even the ears and trotters could be used in stews or soup.

bedroom stew pot

apron colander

firewood iron for clothes

▼ This woman is cooking stew in her cottage.

Life in the Towns

Towns were crowded, unhealthy places in early Victorian times. Smoke from the factory chimneys filled the air.

Workers lived close to the factories. Their houses were damp and crammed close together. People threw their rubbish and dirty water into the street because there were no drains.

▼ People are beginning their day's work in this Victorian street.

laundry woman   pub landlord

milk-delivery boy   slops

▲ The kitchen of a worker's house.

Many houses had a range that was heated by burning wood or coal. It had an oven and hot plates on the top. The family used the range to heat water and cook food. It made the kitchen a cosy place to sit when the day's work was done.

Towns slowly became better places to live. Laws were passed to make them cleaner. Shops and libraries opened. Parks were created. In the evenings, people could enjoy a show at the music hall.

Jobs changed, too. Educated people could work as clerks or teachers. They earned more money than factory workers and lived in bigger houses on the edges of the towns.

range

kettle

washing

bread

iron and stand

hot-water bottle

clothes pegs

frying pan

15

Running the Home

The Victorians thought that all housework was women's work. Even women who had paid jobs did all the housework as well.

Washday was an especially busy day for housewives. This was the day when they washed all the dirty clothes. First, they heated pans of water on the range. Then they scrubbed the dirty clothes with soap on a washboard before rinsing the soap off in a tub. Finally, they hung the washing outside to dry.

▼ This woman is scrubbing clothes on a washboard.

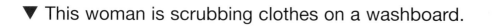

range

pan of hot water

water pump

washboard

tub in sink

carpet beater

▲ This servant works for a wealthy Victorian family. She is dusting some ornaments.

By late Victorian times, many women worked as servants in other people's homes. Some families could only afford to have one servant. Rich families could have more than a hundred.

Victorian homes were not easy to keep clean because coal fires created dust and soot. Maids swept the floors and beat rugs with a carpet beater to get the dust out. They used carbolic soap to scrub floors and keep the steps to the front door spotless.

feather duster

coal fire

gas light

china cups and saucers

teapot

baby's high chair

Washing and Toilets

In early Victorian times, even rich people did not have bathrooms.

Very few homes had running water. Most people had to collect water from pumps in the street. Instead of a sink, people used a jug and a bowl of water for washing.

Most people only had a bath once a week. They would fill a bath with hot water from the range. Then each member of the family would use it. The unlucky person who bathed last got the dirtiest water.

water jug   china basin

soap   shaving jug

shaving brush   cut-throat razor

▼ This man is shaving with a 'cut-throat' razor.

toilet

newspaper

◄ Most families had an outdoor toilet, like this one. They used pieces of old newspaper instead of toilet paper.

Dealing with sewage was a big problem in the towns. Often, several families shared one outside toilet. Sewage was emptied into open pits called cesspools. When sewage got into the water supply, people became very ill. Thousands died.

The answer was to build a network of pipes and tunnels. These carried sewage away from places where people lived.

Pipes were laid to carry fresh water to people's homes, too. By the end of the 1800s, wealthier people had bathrooms, with hot water that came out of a tap.

Shopping for Food

▲ A butcher is weighing some black pudding for his customer.

There were no supermarkets in Victorian times. People bought food from lots of different shops.

The butcher sold all kinds of meat. Hares, ducks, geese and pigeons hung from hooks on the ceiling. These were made into pies or tasty stews. The butcher sold pigs' bladders, too. Children would blow them up and use them as footballs.

hare

goose

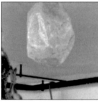

wood pigeons

pheasants

black pudding

pig's bladder

hanging scales

cash register

price in pence

At the grocer's shop, people could buy bread, butter and cheese. Dried food such as flour was kept in big sacks. The grocer weighed it out and put it in a brown paper bag for each customer. Tinned foods, including Heinz Baked Beans, were first sold in late Victorian times.

In some areas, a milkman went around the streets with milk churns on his horse-drawn cart. People brought out jugs to be filled with milk from the churn. There were other street traders, too. They sold everything from fruit and vegetables to meat.

meat pies

Bovril

rabbits

tins

flour sack

stone bottles

▼ This general store sells a wide range of foods.

CHEESE   PURE BUTTER   PURE LARD

Disease and Medicine

poison bottle

medicine bottle

pot of leeches

poultice

herb mixture

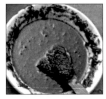

instructions

dried garlic

▲ Herbs were used to make medicines.

Diseases spread easily through the crowded cities. The Victorians did not know what caused most diseases, or how to stop people from getting them.

The Victorians invented all kinds of medicines, but few of them made people better. One common treatment was to put leeches on a sick person's body and let them suck the patient's blood.

Cholera was a disease that killed thousands of people. In 1854, Dr John Snow discovered that cholera was spread when sewage got into drinking water. Other scientists made important discoveries, too, such as how to use antiseptics to kill germs.

► This chemist is making pills. He rolls the mixture into a thin sausage shape and then cuts it into separate pills.

Getting Around

Victorian streets were filled with the sound of horses' hooves and cartwheels.

Many people rode horses to get around. The wealthy travelled in horse-drawn carriages. The first taxis and buses were pulled by horses. Dray horses delivered barrels of beer to pubs from the brewery. Carts carried goods from warehouses to the shops.

▼ Horses were on every town and village street.

carthorse

cobbled street

soap advert

pub

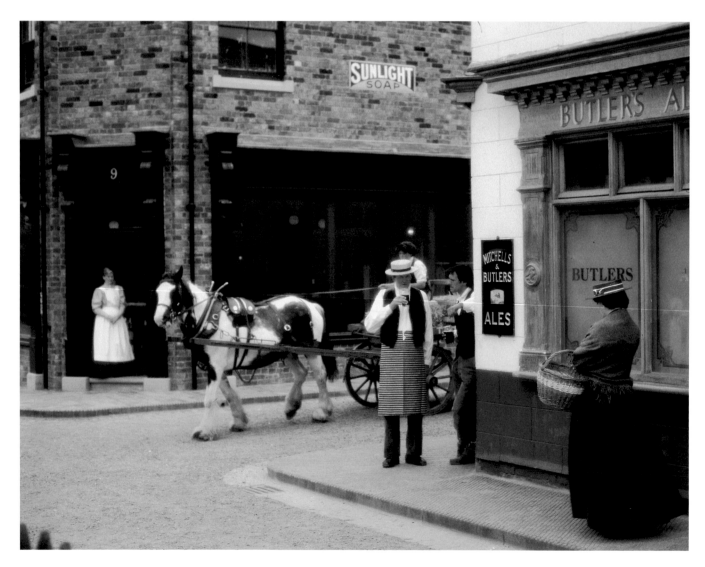

24

▲ A boatman slowly moves his boat through a tunnel.

Horses were not strong enough to pull heavy loads of coal and iron ore. To solve the problem, engineers built artificial rivers, called canals. Heavy loads could be carried by boat instead of by cart.

At first, men pulled the canal boats along with ropes. Later, horses were used. When the canal went through a tunnel, the horse had to be unhitched. The boatman lay on his back and pushed the boat through the tunnel using his legs.

The Railway Age

The first passenger railway opened in Britain in 1825. It ran between Stockton and Darlington, in north-east England. By the time Queen Victoria came to the throne in 1837, railway lines were spreading all over the country.

George Stephenson and his son, Robert, built some of the first railway locomotives. George and Robert Stephenson were great railway engineers. They built huge bridges and blasted tunnels through mountains so that railway lines could be laid.

By the time Queen Victoria died, in 1901, trains were travelling at 55 miles per hour. They became the fastest and cheapest way to move goods over long distances. They were the quickest way for people to travel, too. Factory workers on a day's holiday would cram into the trains for a trip to the seaside. Towns such as Blackpool became popular holiday resorts.

locomotive

carriage

funnel

buffer

steam dome

drive link

driver

cast-iron tracks

▶ A steam locomotive puffs along the railway tracks in Wales.

Timeline

1819

Princess Victoria is born.

1825

First passenger railway opens. It runs between Stockton and Darlington, in north-east England.

1833

The Factory Act says that children under the age of 9 years old must not work in textile factories.

1837

King William IV dies. Victoria becomes queen.

1840

Queen Victoria marries Prince Albert. The Arboretum opens in Derby. It is England's first public park.

1841

Thomas Cook organizes the first railway excursions (day trips).

1842

The Mines Act says that boys under the age of 10 years old must not work underground. No girls or women are allowed to work underground.

1843

Great Britain, the first iron steamship, is launched.

1848

The Public Health Act is passed to try to make towns cleaner and healthier.

1849

Cholera kills 14,000 people in London.

1851

The Great Exhibition is held in London.

1854

Dr John Snow proves that cholera is spread in polluted water.

1865

The first underground sewer tunnels are built in London.

1878

The first electric streetlights are turned on in London.

1880

The Education Act says that all children aged between 5 and 10 years old must go to school.

1887

Queen Victoria celebrates her Golden Jubilee (50 years as Queen).

1890

The Forth Railway Bridge is opened.

1897

Queen Victoria celebrates her Diamond Jubilee (60 years as Queen).

1901

22 January Queen Victoria dies. Her eldest son becomes King Edward VII.

Glossary

Act A law passed by Parliament.

annual A book that is published once a year. Often, it is a collection of stories that have appeared in a comic over the previous 12 months.

antiseptics Chemicals that kill germs.

apprentice A young person who learns a trade by working for an experienced craftsperson.

black pudding A type of sausage made from pigs' blood and fat.

bladder The part of an animal's body that holds waste liquid (urine). It is very stretchy, like a balloon.

cesspools Pits into which people emptied toilet waste and other rubbish.

chamber pot A bowl that people could use instead of going outside to the toilet. They kept it in the bedroom.

cobbled street A street with a hard surface made from rounded stones.

common land Land that many people had the right to use, instead of being owned by one person.

cut-throat razor A razor blade without any kind of safety guard.

dormitory A bedroom that several people share.

dray horse A strong horse used to pull loads.

engineer A person who uses their knowledge of science and maths to design machines, and systems such as canals and railways.

Industrial Revolution A time when the way people lived and worked in Britain changed very quickly. These years of change took place mainly in the late 1700s and the early 1800s.

iron ore Rock that contains iron.

leeches Caterpillar-like creatures that feed on blood.

locomotive An engine that moves.

music hall A theatre that put on shows made up of songs and jokes.

nineteenth century The hundred years between 1801 and 1900.

passenger railway A railway that people can travel on (some railways are only used to carry loads such as coal and stone).

poultice A warm mixture that was spread on the skin to treat infections.

range An oven heated by a fire, with a flat top where pans and kettles are heated.

running water Water that comes from taps in a house.

sewage Waste from toilets.

shoe last Wood or metal model in the shape of a foot, used to mend shoes.

slops Dirty water.

tailor A person who makes and mends clothes.

trotters Pigs' feet.

winding gear Machinery used to bring coal to the surface.

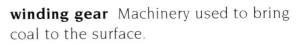

Activities

pp4–5 Who Were the Victorians?

- Ask your parents if they have any old family photographs from Victorian times. You could look for photographs of Victorians in books, too. Put them beside recent photographs of your family. What differences do you notice between the photographs? Compare people's clothes, their expressions and the quality of the photographs.

pp6–7 The Industrial Revolution

- These are some of the places that changed most during the Industrial Revolution: Manchester, Bolton, Bradford, Newcastle, Sunderland, Hartlepool, Birmingham, Derby, Cardiff, Glasgow, London. Find these places on a map of Britain. Trace the map and mark the cities on the map.

pp8–9 Changes at Work

- Design a poster for the printer on page 9 to print. It could be an advert for a shop or a job, or a sign about a lost cat or dog. Look through the other pages of this book for some ideas.

pp10–11 Children at Work

- Think of some adjectives to describe what it might be like to work in an underground coal mine. What might you see? What sounds might you hear? Do you think it would be hot or cold? Write a short poem using as many adjectives as possible.

pp12–13 Life in the Countryside

- Imagine what it might have been like to live in the cottage shown on page 13. What do you think you might have liked about it? What might you have disliked about living there?

pp14–15 Life in the Towns

- Compare the street where you live with the street in the photo on page 14. Look at the buildings, the road and the people. What is similar to your street? What is different?

pp16–17 Running the Home

- Make a list of the machines we use in our homes that run on electricity. (Think about how we prepare and cook food, wash and iron clothes, and clean the house.) What did the Victorians use to do each of those jobs?

- Write a list of instructions for a Victorian maid, telling her all the jobs you want her to do in the house to get it clean.

pp18–19 Washing and Toilets

- Compare the photo of the toilet on page 19 with a toilet in your house. What are the differences? Imagine what it would have been like to go outside every time you had to go to the toilet.

- Joseph Bazalgette was a famous Victorian engineer. Can you find out what he is famous for?

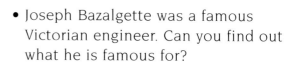

pp20–21 Shopping for Food

- Write a shopping list for food in Victorian times. Include the shop where you will buy each type of food.

- Some of the packaged foods we enjoy today were first sold in Victorian times. Can you find out when these foods first appeared in the shops: Heinz Baked Beans, Cadbury's drinking chocolate, Hovis bread, Tate & Lyle Golden Syrup and Robertson's jam?

pp22–23 Disease and Medicine

- Imagine you are Dr John Snow and you have just worked out how cholera is spread. Design a poster to warn people not to drink polluted water.

pp24–25 Getting Around

- Make up a 'sound picture' for a Victorian town. Think about the sounds you would hear – hooves on the cobbles, traders shouting, water splashing at the pump. Find ways to make the sounds and record them.

- Look at maps of your local area. Were any canals built near you? Are they still used today? What are they used for?

pp26–27 The Railway Age

- Imagine you have just been on a train for the first time. You had never travelled in anything faster than a horse and cart before. Write a diary entry describing how it felt.

Find Out More

BOOKS TO READ

A Victorian Childhood: At Home, At Play, At School, At Work by Ruth Thomson (Franklin Watts, 2007)

Britain in Victorian Times by Tim Locke (Franklin Watts, 2008)

Making History: Victorians by Ann Kramer (Franklin Watts, 2008)

Victorian Life: Clothes by Liz Gogerly (Wayland, 2008)

Victorian Life: Homes by Nicola Barber (Wayland, 2008)

Victorian Life: School by Nicola Barber (Wayland, 2008)

Victorian Life: Transport by Nicola Barber (Wayland, 2008)

PLACES TO VISIT

The Boat Museum, Cheshire
www.canaljunction.com/museum/boat.htm
The photograph on page 25 was taken at this museum, which houses boats and equipment used in Victorian times.

The Black Country Living Museum, Tipton
www.bclm.co.uk/
Many of the photographs in this book, including the street scenes, the chemist's shop and the Victorian kitchen were taken at this museum.

Blists Hill Victorian Town, Shropshire
www.ironbridge.org.uk/
The farm worker's cottage, the shoemaker's shop and the butcher's shop are all part of this recreation of a late-Victorian working town.

Index

History Relived

Contents of titles in the series:

WAYLAND